KINGFISHER READERS

level 2

Amazing Animal Senses

Claire Llewellyn

KINGFISHER

First published 2013 by Kingfisher
an imprint of Macmillan Children's Books
a division of Macmillan Publishers Limited
20 New Wharf Road, London N1 9RR
Basingstoke and Oxford
Associated companies throughout the world
www.panmacmillan.com

Series editor: Heather Morris
Literacy consultant: Hilary Horton

ISBN: 978-0-7534-3089-7
Copyright © Macmillan Children's Books 2013

987654321

1TR/1012/WKT/UG/105MA

A CIP catalogue record for this book is available from
the British Library.

Printed in China

Picture credits
The Publisher would like to thank the following for permission to reproduce their material. Every care has
been taken to trace copyright holders. However, if there have been unintentional omissions or failure to trace
copyright holders, we apologize and will, if informed, endeavour to make corrections in any future edition.
Top = t; Bottom = b; Centre = c; Left = l; Right = r   Cover Shutterstock/mlorenz; Pages 4 Shutterstock/
BlueOrange Studio; 5t Photolibrary/Peter Arnold Images; 5b Shutterstock/mypokcik; 6 Shutterstock/Cathy
Keifer; 7t Shutterstock/Theodore Mattas; 7b Photolibrary/Imagebroker; 8–9 Shutterstock/AnetaPics;
10 Shutterstock/Eduard Kyslynskyy/artwork by Sebastian Quigley; 11 Shutterstock/artwork by Sebastian
Quigley; 12 Photolibrary/OSF; 13t Photolibrary/Tips Italia; 13b Shutterstock/alle; 14 Frank Lane Picture
Agency (FLPA)/Scott Linstead/Minden; 15 Photolibrary/Bridge; 16 Photolibrary/Flirt Collection; 17
Photolibrary/Flirt Collection; 18 Photolibrary/Bios; 19 Photolibrary/Picture Press; 20 Photolibrary/Bridge;
21 Photolibrary/Bios; 22 Shutterstock/Jason S; 23 Photolibrary/Corbis; 24 FLPA/Angela Hampton;
25 Photolibrary/Imagebroker; 26 FLPA/Dembinsky Press Assoc.; 27 Photolibrary/Peter Arnold Images;
28 Photolibrary/Imagebroker; 29 FLPA/Tui De Roy/Minden; 30 Corbis/Jean-Bernard Vernier;
31 Getty/Sandy Huffaker.

Contents

What are senses?

All animals have senses. Senses
tell animals about the world
around them.

Most animals have five senses.
They can see. They can hear.
They can taste. They can smell.
They can touch.

What senses do
people have?

Animal senses

Senses help animals in three important ways.

They help animals to find food.
A frog uses its sight to catch a fly.

Senses help animals to stay safe.
Deer run away when they
hear danger.

Senses help
animals to find
a **mate**. This
bird is singing to
attract a female.

Sense organs

Sense **organs** are parts of an animal's body. They take in signals from the world around them.

These are the sense organs of a dog.

Eyes see what is going on around.

Ears hear sounds.

The nose picks up smells.

Whiskers and skin can touch and feel.

The tongue can taste.

How senses work

Sense organs work with an animal's brain. When a mouse hears a twig snap, a signal travels from its ears to its brain.

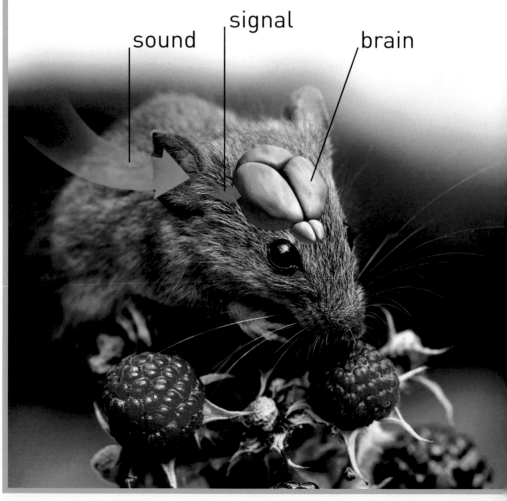

sound

signal

brain

The brain sends a signal to
the legs and the mouse
runs away.

signal

brain

leg

nerves

The signals travel along pathways
called **nerves**. The signals move
very fast.

Sight

How do animals use their sight? They use it to find food and to look out for danger.

A bee sees bright flowers where it can land and feed.

A zebra is always looking out for danger. Its eyes are on the side of its head. It can see all around.

A snail's eyes are on the end of its **tentacles**.

Amazing eyes

An owl has very good sight. It can hunt at night and still see tiny animals on the ground.

The owl's eyes are on the front of its head. This helps it to spot its **prey**.

A dragonfly has huge eyes. Each eye is made up of lots of smaller eyes. This helps the dragonfly to see all around.

Hearing

How do animals use their hearing? They use it to stay safe and **protect** their young.

A hare has very long ears. It can turn them to listen for danger from all around.

Penguins find their chicks by listening for the chick's call.

This is important because there are thousands of other chicks around.

Amazing ears

Elephants have very good hearing.
They can hear
each other
call from
a long way
away.

If an elephant sees a lion, it calls
a warning. Then the **herd** comes
together to protect the young.

Bats squeak as they fly at night. Their squeaks bounce back to them. They hear the **echo** with their big ears. This stops them bumping into things and helps them to catch flying insects.

Taste and smell

How do animals use their taste and smell? They use them to find food and protect their hunting grounds.

A butterfly's taste organs are on its feet. When it lands on a new flower, it can tell if it is good to eat.

Cheetahs mark their hunting grounds with strong-smelling **urine**. When other animals smell the urine, they keep away.

Amazing tongues and noses

Snakes have forked, or fork-shaped, tongues. They flick them in and out to taste the air. This tells them if an animal is near and helps them to find their prey.

Sharks have a very good sense of smell. They can smell a drop of blood from far away. This helps them to find their prey in the dark sea.

Touch

How do animals use their sense of touch? They use it to catch food and find their way around.

A cat uses its whiskers to feel if it can fit through a small gap.

Spiders spin
webs. When an
insect flies into
a web, a spider
feels it shake.
Then the
spider runs to
catch its prey.

Amazing feelers

Some moles have long, pink tentacles on the end of their nose. They are always touching things to see if they are good to eat.

A raccoon has very long fingers.
They help it to feel and catch fish
swimming in the water.

A special sense

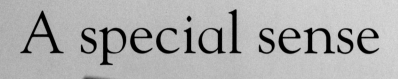

Every year, swallows travel thousands of kilometres to find food and to **breed**. How do they find their way?

They have a special sense that works like a **compass** and tells them where to go.

Turtles have a special sense, too. They can find their way back to the beach where they hatched, to lay their eggs in the sand.

Animals that help us

Some animals help us with their amazing senses.

When people are lost or trapped, search dogs can help find them. The dogs pick up a person's smell in the air and on the ground.

Sea lions have very good sight and hearing. We can train them to find things at the bottom of the sea.

Glossary

breed have babies

compass a tool that helps you to find your way

echo a sound that you hear again when it bounces off something

herd a group of animals that live together

mate the partner an animal has babies with

nerves nerves are like thin wires. They link every part of the body to the brain

organs parts of the body that do special jobs, like eyes and ears

prey an animal that is hunted by other animals

protect to keep safe and out of danger

tentacles long, bendy parts of an animal's body that are often used to touch

urine waste water, or pee, that comes out of the body